DANCING BETWEEN BAMBOO POLES

DANCING BETWEEN BAMBOO POLES

Poetry & Essays

Rebecca Mabanglo-Mayor

For Amanda,

Your words matter.
Thank you for your
dedication to craft
and your friendship.

Cheers! Rebecca
Seattle, July 13,
2019

Dancing Between Bamboo Poles: Poems and Essays

ISBN-13: 978-1-7328636-0-6

Book and cover design by Tonya Namura
Copy editing by Anneliese Kamola.

For Judith, Jill, Steve, and Marie. I'll never forget you.

With deep gratitude for Carol McMillan without whose help this book would not have been published.

Contents

Essays

Poems

The Art of Silencing

"I would have written a shorter letter, but I did not
have the time."   — Blaise Pascal, 1656

For poetry month in 2015, I decided to do a series of
redaction poems. My writing practice felt dry and uninspired,
and my time was limited by a full-time college teaching
position, academic leadership responsibilities, and the usual
tasks of a wife, and mom of two teens. I lacked the discipline
I thought would be required to find and craft words into
readable poems on a daily basis. As a teacher of composition,
however, I already had my editor's skills in the forefront. It
seemed natural to take existing prose pieces and redact words
to create poems.

The plan was simple: find a random passage from a book
plucked from a shelf wherever I found myself. At home,
cookbooks and gardening manuals were likely targets. At my
college office, style manuals and books on culture were the
norm. At the tutoring center, books on science and math
dominated the shelves. Every book was fair game and the
only criterion for choosing a passage was whether a word on
the page caught my attention. Passages had to be at least five
lines long and readable.

Once I found a passage, I copied the page, enlarging the
text for readability. Then I took out my favorite Sharpie pen
and went to work. I allowed myself to redact as many words
as I wanted but required myself to leave at least one word
per line. As the month went on, I found myself particularly
attracted to active verbs and vibrant nouns. The practice
became a game for me to find and keep the best, most

interesting words. In the end, I would review the poem by reading it out loud and redact those few remaining words I thought unnecessary. More than once, I regretted the haste of my Sharpie that obliterated a word I would have rather kept. I resisted the urge to start over. The poems were truly exercises of creativity, experimentation, and surrender.

I posted pictures of the poems on my FB page and didn't think I would do much with them after the end of Poetry Month. In early summer, though, a call for poetry submissions crossed my email and I wanted to participate. The familiar dread of not having the time or creativity to write new work came over me – then I remembered my redaction poems. I reviewed several, chose a few, combined a couple, and edited them further.

To my delight, one poem titled 'muskeg,' a combination of two redactions, was accepted to the anthology *Noisy Water: Poetry from Whatcom County, Washington*.

Redaction poems are similar to found poems in that they reflect the idea that art can be found in the most mundane, unexpected places. Redactions, however, seek to show that a silencing has occurred; if you look closely enough, the missing can be found again. Although my poems began as redactions, they became found poems in the final edits because the redactions are not visible. Occasionally I have added words in parentheses to show they didn't exist in the original texts. Ultimately, the poems I wrote in 2015 reflect my own continuing conversation about silences, something of deep concern in this post-2016 election time. People like me are in fear of being silenced in subtle and violent ways. We fear our histories will be blotted out with black marks of denial and revision. This is one way to look at the future.

The possibility redactions represent culturally, though, is the sense of what was hidden has been revealed. Things overlooked and unseen are voiced because the noise of the expected is silenced. Ideas can find new connections, much like we allies and advocates can find each other to work for a better world despite the shadow that rises before us.

(Original post appeared in the Red Wheelbarrow Writers' blog, Nov. 16, 2016 – http://www.redwheelbarrowwriters.com/blog/the-art-of-silencing/)

muskeg

exposed and scrubby,
proceed north along the wide
coastal landscape covered
with peatlands.
Travel to Prince Rupert,
thread your way, stunted and gnarled,
to large pools of yellow pondweeds snaking
between thick forest of bog laurel and
common juniper in the humid,
subdued slopes of considerable steepness.
Seek muskeg to the west like the Queen, or
Hecate, or Alexander. Find the continuous
Tangle, diverse and mixing with Indian
Hellebore and partridgefoot.

Misapprehension of place, sense of proportion
Lost. A way of seeing predicated on balance.
Move from sight to insight. Create a vision,
an understanding of place.
Creation began a story older than this place,
these steps, that bramble tangle water churn.
Interpretation alone is fitting,
looking away from the light
that is God.

Composed of redactions taken from text found in Plants of the Pacific Northwest
Coast *by Jim Pojar and Andy Mackinnon and* Reasoning Together *edited by
Janice Acoose.*

The Miserable Truth

conditions of retrenchment
noted basics
for less every moment
austerity wars.

"settling" is pervasive
to the present   an unusual
program
illustrates constancy of settling

mini-histories
tell tales of cockroaches, tiny and
constant
through changes,
implement theories about
which program (will)
prevail.   Hephzibah
notes difficulties
lay in directors
requiring them to assume "a
practice"
to ensure continuing
status   humorous fashion, the
heroic efforts, secure pay due them, acquire
floodwaters. But those efforts
virtually guarantee

The Orwellian "subordinate-but-equal" position
"conditioning" delimita-
tions, a challenge to
individual's own risk.
the "fittest" sort
precisely to endure
such conditions: someone who "fits."

Composed of redactions taken from text found in Representing the Other *by
Bruce Horner and Min Zhan Lu.*

Trespassing

So ancient is attributing a difficult
common past with borders which have moved with conquest.
North and South share varieties which differ only regionally.
Garbures and melted cheese have a common
heritage left by domination, the trade of crops exposed
by the wake of Christopher Columbus and his single
revolutionary event.

"Native" means merely "before there" to the question
"What is Native?" "What is imported?"
No inconsiderable number of cursory tales
reveal how and when importation occurred
over many routes, circled the globe East
to West, like germs widespread, before
the arrival of "civilization" and "culture."
A specific case: coastal towns feared raids
long before white feet,
conflicts with pirates imbue the legends

Conquest, persuasive and pervasive in its instruction,
charts its own course
landscaping generations.

Composed of redactions taken from text found in The Old World Kitchen *by Elizabeth Luard and* Filipino Folktales *by Dean Fansler.*

truffle voices

snobbish attitude   valued too often
        Colette   Apicius, Pliny
irresistibly simple
advising the penurious
truffle peelings. "Naturally all other
genuinely fresh.
Butter from Normandy,
and if possible   with a slight tang
rather than
an aphrodisiac, a no-nonsense skeptic can't
resist twitting   expect
the provider of truffles
provider of panhaggerty
or of haggis and bashed neeps.
Abundant whisky cannot be claimed
for any food."

Composed of redactions taken from text found in The Mushroom Feast *by*
Jane Grigson.

Extrapolating

spectacular successes
of various
forms of genetic statements
have tended toward exuberant,
unlimited control, and led to
blueprinting of human personalities,
more restrained second thoughts.

Nevertheless, alarms have caused
concern and threaten global
technological advances.
Who would wish man's
inner nature? Indeed fear may arouse even more
death. The mass media welcomed
seasonal pronouncements,
while it seems clear that
drama help(s)
radical changes in our
social structure and
improve(s) our protection against harmful
exaggeration of a
distorted public view,
ignores its contributions to our welfare. Irresponsible

hyperbole has already influenced funding.
It seems important to assess objectively
the pattern of
principles that must be taken into account.

Composed of redactions taken from text found in Writing in the Disciplines *by Mary L. Kennedy; William J. Kennedy; and Hadly M. Smith.*

Discrete Phenomena

discrete techniques of many
phenomena are included in text(s),
recursion, growth, and Markov
chains.

Contemporary applications designed to encourage
new and innovative
themes to ask familiar
questions. Each
spiral has an effect on the instruction by
no more than regularly
having discussions to ask and
answer "What if...?" to conjecture, to check guesses and
to work with real activities, invaluable contributions
to process(es)

developed in many diverse areas
sciences are included, models from
anthropology, economics, sociology sport
complexity and depth,
new techniques(.)

For example, characteristics
are investigated and applied. Later
phenomenon of growth assist in
the consideration of long-run expectation.

(D)esigned for a head-down march, the
work to create additional questions and reflection
no single "best"
answer   constructed with philosophy   the quality of
learning is more important than the completion.

Composed of redactions taken from text found in Contemporary Precalculus *by Gloria B. Barrett et al.*

Cultural Survival

"Preserving our identities" is an easy answer
to defend purity against "mongrelization."

Most people are not racists.
The answer is not white,
not capitalist either, nor produced
by people whose impeccable cultural identity
is the problem.

The people most opposed to identity aren't
much interested in the real-life versions of
the fictional ones, which are, at best
intemperate remarks by chickens who cling
to a concept that has "ever-widening circulation."

The answer to "who are we?" is increasingly
the assertion of cultural identity,
an indigenism, an interconnectedness
predating common time and reaching toward
an undetermined future.

Composed of redactions taken from text found in The Trouble with Diversity *by Walter Benn Michaels.*

Memory Bank

We have to
preserve this knowledge
about our biosphere, our biodiversity to keep
going, to make sure it's alive.

(T)he enthosphere of human creativity
a way to continue (a)
legacy of living sustainably with different
landscapes   when we lose
specific ecosystems

the landscape is not going to work
and visa versa,
the context and their moral metaphors.
landscapes, referred to
as journeys across a landscape, (are)
to find our own cognitive landscapes,
this land adopted.

(We) find on that
way (to) the plants. Connect with them
then your metaphors will begin

place becomes your moral landscape.

Composed of redactions taken from text found in Original Instructions *edited by Melissa Nelson.*

Sun and Soil

nothing more than
chervil, sweet woodruff, and sorrel,
lovage and lemon balm –
require at least half; appreciate more.

light, slow growing, spindly,
unhappy you choose
full sun in June,
are there any
that will season and shade, or
overtake them?

next in importance, a perfect world,
loamy, sweet, often described as chocolate.
we're sometimes given stale bread – too sandy and dry.
heavy soil can be fussy. Your
poppies may wither in conditions
fairly easy going.

However, it is paramount that good, no matter what –
feel tortured if they have to live
standing constantly around   more susceptible
to rot and perish, particularly if
winter fatalities don't come where they should

hardy, wet or sporadic
the ground remained   the insulation of
a better chance.

Composed of redactions taken from of text found in The Herb Farm
Cookbook *by Jerry Traunfeld.*

Everywhere Is Nowhere

reviving heirloom and
traditional varieties of
onslaught
defined "good" as
higher yields and
those traits   corrupt in and of itself
at the expense of   varieties
that could not make the grade.

the more
commodities that simply
suggest
what
I dismiss out of hand

an apple
is a nice thing.
healthy and   traits are good
things
particularly (in) self-selecting
conditions   normally late
my early fruit

Something
supported my personal agenda
chill comes

who am I to disregard the logic?
I object to those who have hijacked it.

Composed of redactions taken from text found in A Householder's Guide to the Universe *by Harriet Fasenfest.*

A body suspended

in stable equilibrium
vertically below its suspension
represents
the center of
two different points,
its center of gravity   no matter
its orientation.

Taking two steps, we
write

Sigma tau equals r sub cm by Mg

The torque on the body equals
the single force Mg
and thus the
gravity coincides with
the second assertion
that *gravity*
of a body is zero.

conditions
in equilibrium show that
a single
center of mass
will be zero, for equilibrium
the body will be
any point

through the net
in this case because
of action. We can therefore balance
only at the center
any point directly *below* or *above*
center

Composed of redactions taken from text found in Physics, 4th Ed, Vol. 1 *by Resinck, Halliday, and Rane.*

Results from *unreliable questions*

admit doing things that others
disapprove of.   reliability is
          two-way   question
                    contexts   the threat of
criminism   choose the
lowest   or none at all   better to
question   to name
                    a range.   assume
          the behavior
          may sound like an accusation
          be tempted to answer "No"
                    without
          more accurate answers
          potentially threatening
          behavior of others
to find   members of a group

          directly
                    loading

                              questions   in the bias of the
questioner   to produce biased answers.
the defense of our country
suggests a "no" from someone
unconcerned with

as unpatriotic, most
would be "Yes"

crucial to the validity of
writing
keep it short, word your
information   and check your bias.

Composed of redactions taken from text found in The Bedford Guide to the
Research Process, 2nd Ed. *by Jean Johnson.*

job security

having the best
Judgments made on
children is not necessarily
who we recognize.
(D)edicated service
would be
categorized on the basis of subject
separations
made
in a particular area   the last
hired were math teachers and layoffs were
apportioned among
the least

one system
with strong union opposition
would terminate the weak
require
guards to ensure
ability – or lack thereof –
hence
There are no easy
answers   save someone
unsettle lives of all

accommodation has to be reached to
be better

Composed of redactions taken from text found in For Our Children: A Different
Approach to Public Education *by Frank Macchiarola and Thomas Hauser.*

Sensitivity tests

such cases may be analyzed by methods
for others or by
an assumption of
normality   rough but quick for the
critical   plot   of items explod-
ing   commercially

a straight line by eye
suggest a transformation
give approximate normality
fitting more precisely
a measure   more efficient

when they   are recommended
the effect   is known immediately
readily adjusted
the charge   described
is not practical

the ultimate effects
are   measured on   small animals, such as
hamsters or mice. If it is inconvenient
tests of rockets is
appropriate for detailed application
and reliability.

Composed of redactions taken from text found in Statistics Manual *by Edwin L.*
Crow, Frances A. Davis, and Margaret W. Maxfield.

Spark

spark personal transformation
recognize the different ways
many people have led
(r)eflections and (how) the present (c)ommunity
work from projects
and obvious practice.

(W)omen shelter
narratives
in community   learn the socio-cultural
situated knowledge,
strategies(.)   (T)eachers
reflect on how shame, embar-
rass(ment), and anger flower
dialogue to structure
a lead collaborative
(p)arenthood.

Sexuality and relationship(s,)
while
local(ly) public(,) have transformed
practices such as
mentoring, reading, and constructing multi-voiced
research reports and school-
based arguments in classrooms. In doing so they
face and negotiate pressures to conform.

Composed of redactions of text found in Writing and Community
Engagement *by Thomas Deans, Barbara Rosswell, and Adrian J. Wurr.*

Any number

(T)he wickedness of designing matters less
whether
the artifact
might access the Web.
An immersive response
to realize the goal
and the responsibility for
(t)he design task(.)

(C)reate a manipulable
artifact from which a topic
is not the advice; it is not
the artifact. Instead create
a quite familiar
promise on any
topic from dating to fashion.
These artifacts are less aware,
those features conditioned.
(A)ny audience must respond
at every level and at every step
manipulate the features.

(T)hey function to actually
think about the features of the
audience(. T)heir artifacts
steer them in terms of
a number of viable artifacts(.)

(O)ne example used
answers to questions that lead them
to join the military(.)
This artifact was not
any single question.
(T)he series can be led down different
paths. (I)mages paired on any given frame contributed
to the gravity of decision.

Composed of redactions taken from text found in Multimodal Composition:
A Critical Sourcebook *by Clair Lutkwitte.*

this interconnectedness

a net or web: (s)nip one
because all the
connections are
just one thing.

(M)ultipurposeness
plays many roles — a quality
designed from
the typical
intended to serve(,)
chosen for
restrain(ed,) unruly
play(.)

(C)apable of
much work, prone to
a lusher, richer
shade. Can't it offer
both people and wildlife
fruit
more heavily? Plus
harvest rainwater and
build soil   they fall already
doing fifteen different
"yields" to other parts

Composed of redactions taken from text found in Gaia's Garden *by Toby Hemenway.*

Biocentrism

Being Mora
entities
it is
good that
all living creatures, given
beneficence in morality
locates
drives, aims (toward)
growth and natural fulfillments

yet inconsistently
restricts the bearers of
sentient creatures
understanding
biocentrism.   (C)arefully distin-
guish belief in sentience
and the view
from
all holders, sentient or nonsentient,
(who) have the same significant. On that basis,
life would be unlivable.

Constructed from redactions taken from text found in The Encyclopedia of Environmental Ethics and Philosophy, Vol. 1, *J. Baird Calliott and Robert Frodeman, Chief Eds.*

Sound

at the beginning of
chance gives speakers
who pronounce
in terms of
structure and would
supplement language as a basis
to organize
themes like clothing, weather, food,
a living set of values
and customs.

A substantial number (of)
children take traditional
lessons to clear many facets
made relevant today.

(T)he story of an elder
about the contrast between
when she was young and today.
(F)amily and kinship play
in the child, and include
views of health. (E)lders
mentioned the culture to sound
like mother(-)teaching.

(D)iscovering
(m)y preference would explain
how rules apply to

the approach   most
report
language(,)
helpful verbal paradigms(,)
designed to reflect a style(,)
emphasizes observation.

(A)dmit it was difficult for
succinct explanations appropriate for
the audience, partly anxious
about a book that does not conform(.)

(L)anguage knows
and I do not.

Composed of redactions taken from text found in Indigenous Language Revitalization *edited by Jon Reyhnerand and Louise Lockard.*

Additive Style

the additive style
of associative nonconnectedness is
antithetical to you

raise the issue, but put off taking
a few more examples

acknowledge influence on another
style –
less philosophical and
mainly from famous
pieces of
Anglo-Saxon words

leave yourself out
be realistic
hardboiled, spare, and lapidary

two words are particularly apt
transparency
attention
self-effacement
allows the beauty
by paring away layers

not
excessive

claim the thing itself.

Composed from redactions of text found in How to Write a Sentence and How to Read One *by Stanley Fish.*

Hemp stalk is the form

unfounded.
New tech can form smoke,
madness,
mystique.
Users know danger, hear
upon
why
ban
HE

essential resource
more durable
grow fast
eliminate need
woo
solve political, economic, environmental problem
reason why
produce time as bulk   source of food
in crops can
nation
it does deplete oil
make paint lubricant
new fuel
adapt to climates.

Composed of redactions taken from text found in The Writer's Way *by Jack Rawlins and Stephen Metzger.*

color and form

perhaps woven through
color and form   informal or highly staged
spell out
to accommodate
more progression
maturing
between
mid- to late-summer

the space left empty
near the house

appreciate delicious
summer nights
that freely release fragrance – rosa rugosa
nasturtium, mockorange, honeysuckle, and
lilies   all so power-
fully scented
an infinity be-
yond the scope
brushed against
and creeping

tough enough to withstand
[within reason]

Constructed from redactions taken from text found in The Moosewood
Restaurant Kitchen Garden *by David Hirsch.*

first glance

individuals hunt more than
6 and 7
days [Unfortunately
successful] but
did not hunt more
in 1967.

kill is not greater than
24 percent on
seasonal kill taken into account

seven western states
regrettably adds to
the confusion.   total kill
are greater than average
per hunt
however, the divergence
stems from the water

inquire about
all forms of hunting.   estimate
indirectly the total through simple
expansion   say they hunt;
conclude that
hunters are more conscientious
in the response and
overestimate the total number

because queries
buy federal stamps

a group which often includes substantial
individuals not required to
"kill" rather
"retrieve"
circumvent all these difficulties
to state estimates comparable
to distortions in
plausible adjustments

success seems
useless to belabor

Constructed from redactions taken from text found in Waterfowl and
Wetlands: Toward Bioeconomic Analysis *by Judd Hammack and Gardner
Mallard Brown.*

search for gold

build
many roads and trails in the Pacific
Northwest

gold fever reached coastal
centers   gold found near
the development of northeastern
facilities and the usual
separation of miners explained
trouble
brought on
(b)ecause of the
gold   little mining
occurred after 1858   peace was
the first gold established

but the gold turned out
by a group of sailors of insignificant value
were important
mines in
northward
waters

they discovered
founded the boom town
to become (t)erritory
made in traces of

gold a tributary
following
French Flats and Kirby

gold was discovered
with the Pierce party
and, a little later, on Applegate
Creek and the Rogue River   within a year
these discoveries
became the creek named
Oro Fino "fine
gold"

Composed from redactions taken from text found in Our Pacific Northwest *by Chester D. Babcock and Clare Applegate Babcock.*

One Story

Myself proceeds
too smoothly.
Each day, it was possible to cover
my mistakes.
The illusion of virtue comes easily.

However,

(t)he discussion that followed began to emerge,
reminding, it seemed, the reasons for sadness
before hope.

One woman recalls shame
unfamiliar and unappealing.
A beauty
to pay for
humiliation
and blighted days.

In a rural area,
she could finally begin to tell her story.
How destructive it is
yell out
"Boy!"
to feel the young man's anger.

Composed of redactions of text found in The Kindness of Children *by Vivian Gussin Paley.*

In Vastness

Practitioners of water, the sum of all flow,
glinting dew, shimmering sea foam, frozen
ice sheets need the open spaces of deep valleys,
trenches between ocean mountains, swales or
sloughs, cricks and creeks, even thumbprints,
to bear witness to the shifting rhythms of creation,
the dissolution of canyons, the flooding fields,
the tender berry shoots, the calving whales.

Appeal to the emotions, the waters that move reason
to foolishness and shift drab, humorless subjects
into wonder – a cat's eye green, a spiderweb strung
between silver bumpers, orange-yellow lava cascading
from mountain birth to sea death – thousands of markers
beyond the beaver in the marsh, beneath a clasp of stars,
into desired depths where compulsion overrides
the sensibility of a life lived safely.

Once a young man in a small town barbershop left
a message: My Pledge – work, save, sacrifice, endure.
The whole struggle, the kind of renunciation we are all
called upon to make. Our best effort, our single-mindedness
separate us from the problems we confront. And yet
the diversity borne of water compels us beyond
boundaries of lives within steel and concrete, asphalt
and fossil fuels, to seek those who still remember water.

Composed of redactions taken from the text A Sequence for Academic Writing
by Laurence Behrens and Leonard J. Risen.

Essays

Becoming A Woman Of Color

Imagine.

A rustle of bedclothes, a shift in the mattress. Your three-year-old daughter is trying not to fall asleep.

"Do you like Christopher Robin?"

Eyes closed, you smile and decide not to scold her.

"Yes, I like Christopher Robin very much. He's a nice boy."

"Christopher Robin's not a boy. Christopher Robin is a girl. She has a round head."

"And girls have round heads?"

"Yes, that's right. And boys have...?"

"Boys have long heads. Right!"

You open your eyes to darkness and try to remember how things used to be so simple and wonder when her world will change.

Remember.

The sticky feel of fresh green beans as you try to snap them. You sit with your mother at the kitchen table and your legs dangle above the yellowed linoleum.

Your mother does not need to watch her fingernails bite the ends off the beans and break the green flesh into perfect bite-sized pieces. Instead, she watches your grandmother pace the kitchen floor, first stirring a pot, then washing a dish, and shares your latest news.

"She helped a new boy in school with his school work," says your mother as another bean falls in half. "His mother thanked me for bringing up such a thoughtful child. But I told this girl to be careful of those boys. We never know what they really want."

You try to watch your mother's fingers to understand how she is able to keep the broken ends in her curved palm and still snap beans cleanly. You look at the mess you've made of the bean in your hand, ends smashed, its center mangled and oozing.

"Hiya," she says, taking the bean and snapping its remains into edible pieces. "Don't waste food."

You hear your grandmother say something in a Filipino dialect and you think she has said something about America not being the same as back home. You think you see your mother glance at you when she doesn't answer your grandmother right away, but when you look up at her, she is taking the tin colander of beans to the sink and begins to run the water.

"That's enough for now," she says as water drains through tiny holes. "Go see if your cousins are here yet."

As you walk through the kitchen door, you hear your grandmother clicking her tongue.

"Ah, *sayang*" she says. "So sad. Too much yet to learn."

Remember the Rules.

Girls must be polite, generous, demure, deferential, especially to men and old people, but be intelligent. Nobody likes a dumb girl.

Girls must take piano and ballet lessons but should not be ballerinas or pianists. Artists starve, you know.

Girls are not expected to excel in math or science, but excel anyway. You may have to support yourself one day.

Girls do not drive cars, only their fathers or husbands drive them, especially on freeways. Anyway, where do you have to go during the week that can't wait until the weekend?

Above all, remember.
Girls must stay out of the sun. You are the daughter of professionals, not field workers.

Picture grade school.
You wore the red, white, and blue uniform of your parochial school, and the nuns there did not wear penguin black habits. Instead, they wore polyester housecoats, hand sewn on the weekends, or brown-and-gold pantsuits found at the St. Vincent de Paul Thrift Shop. Not a heavy wood rosary or ruler to be found among them, but you knew that a trip to Sister Patricia's office meant a spanking from hands thick as a ream of paper.

It was Sister Patricia who called the school to a general assembly. All six grades squeezed into the three narrow hallways forming a *T* at one end of the school. The younger ones from the Primary Grades lined in front of the taller Intermediates. You are short for an Intermediate and it is hard to see, so you trace the trails of mortar in the brick wall with your finger and listen to Sister's voice. Somewhere in the crowd you figure your best friends are already planning what to do at lunchtime.

First, you all recite the Pledge of Allegiance to the flag and then the Pledge of Allegiance to the Cross. Then come the announcements and you hear something about a war overseas and boat people (like people living on houseboats in Seattle?) and how you should make the newcomer feel welcome. There is murmuring and a shift in the crowd and you think you see someone moving forward to be presented. You brace yourself against the wall and stand tiptoe, but all you can see is the top of a boy's head, black and shiny. You move your head to the right and you see a bit of his red sweater, lumpy on one side, and the edge of his white shirt dislodged from his black pants. Sister's thick hand rests on his head and you hear the others murmur something about him being in your class.

He doesn't matter much to you, and you settle back on your heels. He's from Asia somewhere and you can tell he's not going to be very smart. You figure he can't speak English very well, so he won't be bugging you for math help. Hopefully, none of the Sisters will ask you to buddy up with him; you've got better things to do with your time.

Finding a flaw on a brick, you finish tracing the mortar and wonder if there will be a game of spoons at lunchtime.

Remember another bed, another time.

The crunch of paper beneath your body, the slick coolness of the ultrasound wand as it slides along your belly. You peer at the monitor and try to decipher the image made of black and white streaks across the screen. You see the heart beating strong, see the head unimaginably large, see a thumb finding its way to a mouth.

"Are you sure you want to know?" the tech asks.

You look at your husband and smile. You're trying not to hope it's a boy. You're trying to be open to any sex. This is your baby after all.

"Everything look okay?" he asks.

You listen as the tech runs through the standard markers for a healthy second-trimester fetus. You find yourself trying not to check whether there is a penis on the monitor.

"So, it's a..." You hesitate in case your nonchalant voice cracks.

"Very healthy girl. Congratulations."

You try to smile and check the monitor again in case she was wrong.

Remember.

A park bench with peeling brown paint. Your hand clenched in your lap.

"I can't do it. I can't do this. A girl."

"Honey, you'll be fine. You'll make a terrific mother."

Tears mix with mist from the lake. You wish you had a few crumbs to feed the swans. You wonder where the muskrat is and try to find his trail on the surface of the water.

"I don't know anything about being a girl, about being a woman. A boy —" you hiccup. "You could bring up such a wonderful boy."

This man who is your husband curves his arm around your shoulders. You think of all the things he has been. Eagle Scout. Drum Major. Scientist.

You, this woman who is now a mother, swings your feet like a child. You think of all the things you've never been. Never a cheerleader. Never a Prom Queen. Never boy-crazy.

Wonder what this poor girl-to-be did to deserve a woman like you.

Picture your parents.

"You may have been born in America, but you are a Filipina. Never forget that."

You stare at your father as he stands over you, jabbing the air between the two of you with his finger. Your mother hovers somewhere behind him, looking for something in the cabinets, a snack maybe, or something to drink. You can tell she somehow doesn't agree with what he is saying, thinks that it is futile to argue the point. At least that's what you hope. You need an ally right now, someone to explain why you do the things you do that make your father crazy.

"Are you listening? You must respect your parents, do you hear me?"

You will not nod. You will not concede. You know you are right. You want to say, What is wrong with being an American anyway? You came here, you had me here. Not in the Philippines.

"We came here, we sacrificed for you. And this is what you do?"

Your jaw is clenched and now you are trying not to cry. It does not matter what you have done this time, you've heard this lecture before. You look to your mother again. She ducks her head and picks up a glass from the dish-drainer.

"She doesn't know," your mother says to him, placing the glass carefully in the cupboard. "She wasn't brought up like back home."

By the set of his shoulders, you can see he isn't listening. Or at least, he's trying not to listen, because after a moment his glare softens. He turns and leaves, tugging his reddened ear, mumbling something in Tagalog.

"Give up," she says, giving you a glass of water. "You cannot win, *hiya*. He is your father."

You sit back in your chair and stare at the almond Formica of the countertop. You want to scream out loud, I am not a Filipino. I am not fresh off the boat. I am not from Cambodia, or Japan, or China, or Korea. I was born in Seattle.

I am an American.

Remember filling out affirmative-action forms your freshman year in college.

You look for a place on the pale blue form to put your name or birthplace. You can't find a space for the name of your high school or how high you ranked among your classmates. Not even a place for you to write in your major or career plans. Instead, a column of boxes and designations flows down the page and, at first glance, you don't seem to belong anywhere on the form.

You know you are not blind, hard of hearing, physically disabled in any way. You figure glasses are no big deal and leave the first section alone. You know you've never been in a war, Vietnam or otherwise, so you skip the next two sections about mental disabilities or disabilities associated with being a veteran. You figure the form is just for tracking statistics or maybe identifying people who need special help. You doubt that the form will help you get good grades in your advanced Physics or Math classes.

You skip over the question about being over 40 and nearly return the form with only "Woman" checked off. You feel strange to even mention being a woman, because you feel healthy enough and how could being a woman be a disadvantage?

At first, your think the last section with the race categories doesn't relate to you. After all, you're an American Citizen, not a foreign-exchange student. But you hesitate, feeling that your one check box isn't enough.

You let your pencil hover over the boxes: Hispanic – if Hispanic, Chicano, Latino or Mexican. Black. Native American – designate tribal affiliation. Asian/Pacific Islander. You see there's no box for Filipino, and you're not sure you'd check that box anyway. Your parents are Filipino, but you were born in Seattle. Your hands begin to sweat and you feel as if you're failing the last test to make your college entrance final.

You go through the list again, and try to find a box to check. You know you are not Black nor have a tribal affiliation, and you skip those boxes. Your mother was a Hidalgo before she married, but does that make you Hispanic? You suspect your father has Chinese in his background, but does that make you Asian? And Pacific Islanders are only from Hawaii, right?

You want to walk away, toss the blue sheet of paper in the trash, but it looks too official, and you stop. You tap your pencil to your forehead then check a box.

Your advisor stares at you when you tell her about the form and how confusing it was. You can see that she would have known what boxes were right for you.

Imagine.

Your daughter is in love with the color pink. You never intended her to be a pink girl, in fact you carefully avoided too much of the pale color when she was a baby. You wanted her to love all the colors: bright, primary colors. Frills were impractical, especially in the Honolulu heat. But today she must wear pink. And lots of it. Pink socks, pink shirts, pink pants, pink sweater, pink boots, pink hat, pink coats. She's swimming in pink and if there is no pink to be worn, watch out, there will be no consoling her. Buy multiples of everything in pink, especially socks. She will concede to white undershirts and diapers, but everything else must be pink.

"I'm pink!"

You smile, ever indulgent. "Yes you are, honey."

"I'm pink and Papa is pink," she says pointing to herself and her father somewhere behind her. She frowns. "But you're brown."

"Yes, sweetheart." You hold your hands behind your back to keep them from trembling.

"And your hair is black. My hair is not black."

"No, it's brown, like Papa's." You feel muddy and outside the alignments your daughter is making.

"Pink! I love pink. Do you like pink, Mama?"

"Yes, yes I do." Because pink is her favorite color.

Remember.

The priest during your final wedding-preparation interview. He is nervous as he rubs his hands over his knees and you know he is trying to form the next question. His face turns a deep reddish purple and his voice is barely above a whisper.

"I have to ask you this question." He swallows and looks at your fiancé. "Have you discussed...how...well, that you're...I mean...that you're a mixed couple?"

You look at your fiancé for clarification and see that he looks as confused as you are. You know he wants you to speak; after all, you have more experience in this Catholic stuff.

"But Father." You speak slowly to be sure you have the words right. "Father, he was Methodist before, but now he's converting, so we're okay, right?"

You swallow, hoping there isn't a loophole in Catholic Canon that you've missed.

Remember.

Your mother on a weekend just before the wedding, her arms crossed as if to keep her body together. She has just finished saying how wonderful your fiancé is, and you can tell she is trying to say something indirectly. Again.

"I just want to know...I mean, maybe I should have pushed you more. But you were so young. To you know... date your own kind."

You try not to look deflated. This old story again. You want to ask why, what was forgotten that was so important now. Why had she and your father moved to Federal Way,

Washington, where there were no other Filipinos in your neighborhood? You want to say how Filipino men all look like your cousins and although you once wanted to marry your favorite childhood cousin, you've gotten over him and the others now. To date a Filipino, well, it just seemed too much like incest.

You want to tell her that you have nothing in common with Filipinos, you can't speak the language, you can't cook the food, you can't tell the jokes. You went to school with Americans, went to Mass with Americans, sang in choir with Americans, why wouldn't you marry one?

Instead, you shrug.

"Too late, I guess," she says smoothing the front of her sweater. "He's a nice boy. I like him. Besides, children of Asians and whites are so beautiful."

Picture your daughter.

Your parents will call her Kulasi-si Puting-puti. Little white bird. You will know by the repetition of syllables that the name is not just "white" but "white-white," very white.

"Strong genes," your relatives will comment on her baptismal day, and they will look at your husband with suspicious admiration.

You tell yourself it's because she was two months premature, that she will darken with time, that her fine hair will thicken and darken. You try not to remember that these are the same reassurances you whispered to yourself as you nursed her in the NICU when she was only three days old. You will block from your thoughts the image of your dark daughter being switched with a lighter baby,

by accident of course, because it was a full moon the day
she was born and the emergency room was busy. You will
not look suspiciously at your husband, and try to banish
the thought that she is only his child, not yours, somehow,
even though you were very much present when she
entered the world.

She will be able to pass in ways you had only imagined
you could. You've passed for Native American, East Indian,
Hawaiian, even Korean, but she will pass as white. You
only imagine yourself as white, try to believe it doesn't
matter that you are not white.

You do not even know you are passing until you live
in Honolulu, where there are faces like yours everywhere,
on TV, at the mall, on Da Bus. And then you become
a stranger to your own skin. People can see you were
Filipina and speak Tagalog to you as if you can understand.
They ask if you were your daughter's nanny and murmur
Hapa when you say you are her mother.

Hapa. Half and half.

Not you. Not yours.

Imagine.

A shift on the living room couch, the feel of tiny hands
climbing your legs on their way to your lap. You open your
eyes and try to keep your daughter from sitting on your
enlarged stomach.

"How's the baby?" she asks, patting your arm.

"Growing every day, just like you."

"Just like me?" she looks to the ceiling and weighs your
words. "Will the baby like pink?"

"Maybe."

"I like pink." She looks down at her hand. "I'm pink and Papa's pink."

"Yes." You hesitate, feeling the next beat of her litany.

"You're brown. And your hair is black. Will I be brown when I grow up?"

"I don't know, *hiya*. We'll have to wait and see."

"Is the baby pink like me or brown like you?"

"It's too soon to tell."

"Is it a boy like Papa or a girl like me?"

You shake your head and shrug.

Your daughter pushes at the hem of your sweater. "Let me see." You push the waistband of your maternity pants down a bit to satisfy her. As she settles next to you, you wonder if she can see something you cannot. Humming softly, she smiles and lays her pale hand on your dark skin.

Gift of Plums

When summer days begin to wane toward Fall, it's hard to stay indoors. It must have been that way for my dad those Sunday afternoons in the early '70s, when he would turn our big blue Coronet 500 sedan out of the church parking lot in the opposite direction of home. He spent his workdays verifying invoices and his nights balancing the family checkbook or watching the football game on TV. Saturdays were his garden days, pulling up weeds and mending bean trellises. Even on Sundays chores needed to be done, but only if he drove straight home after Mass. Maybe the sunlight would strike his face as he left the church and he'd breathe deep the offshore wind, then it would be settled in his mind. No chores today.

He and Mom settled themselves on shiny leather bucket seats, and me in the back, the seat all to myself. I was probably nine or so and if I stretched out and lay down on the seat, my head and feet would never touch the door, the seat was so wide. Old Thumper, as we called my dad's car. It didn't have air conditioning, so we'd roll down the windows and let the air billow in. Warm air, that didn't so much cool, but moved the air around, made us feel a little bit better than the closeness of a car shut from the world.

When we hit the corner of Old 99 and 320th, Dad would tap his wedding band on his left hand in counterpoint to the rhythm he tapped with his class ring on his right hand, and we'd wait for the light to change from red to green. I'd try to guess our destination from where he steered the car next – east meant Auburn and the search for fresh fruits and vegetables at old truck farms that dotted the valley. South meant visiting cousins in Tacoma, while north usually meant visiting my mother's parents in Seattle. Any direction, though, meant a long ride by my nine-year-old reckoning, and I'd doze, listening to my parent's conversation weave in and out of songs on the radio.

My parents spoke Tagalog, a Filipino dialect with rolling tones that rose and fell around and through the strains of "Stranger in Paradise" and "How Much is that Doggie in the Window." As I drifted to sleep, their voices mixed with the drone of tires on pavement, turned hollow and distant, then melted into dreams of yellows and pinks and greens. Often I'd wake in time to hear my dad shut off the engine and see the world in shades of blue, the brightness of waking up too much for me at first. Blinking, I'd sit up, peering up and out through the window to see where we'd arrived.

Sometimes I'd find us in front of a low-slung Craftsman with a simple porch and picture window facing the street. Stepping out of the car, I'd get quieter inside myself, cautious in unfamiliar surroundings. My parents, on the other hand, would be excited and smiling, knocking carefully at the door, then opening it if it was unlocked. I'd follow them into a small foyer, then through the dining room of the darkened house. Like a closed-up car, the room felt hot and cramped, the dark wood furniture and the scent of mothballs giving the space an unlived-in feel. The voices rose and fell again as my parents exchanged greetings with the owners of the house. I heard "Auntie Dora!" and "How big you are!" and "Are you hungry?" and my caution turned into a feeling of boredom as I realized there were no other children in this house, and it would be adults talking over and around me in a language I didn't speak.

But as dark as the house was inside, the terraced back yard was always bright and sunny. A small kitchen garden was grown on the first level nearest the kitchen – peas and corn, tomatoes and squash, spinach and bok choy. Then down the next terrace were the trees, three plum trees and one apple tree, each bursting with fruit. Actually, they weren't plum trees but Italian prune trees, which always confused me a bit because to my mind prunes were those oversized wrinkly raisins my mother complained about having to eat every so often because she felt "a bit stopped up." And come to think of it, Italian prunes, in the garden of a Filipino, they could probably be called anything we wanted. So they were The Plums, oval and dusty purple, soft and sweet. Small, too. I could eat one in two bites, carefully avoiding the seed for my mother's sake.

Uncle Sammy, Auntie Dora's husband, handed Dad a white bucket, and he trudged down the hill to fill it. Their conversation wouldn't lose a beat as Uncle Sammy trailed behind, stopping occasionally to pull up a bunch of plantain growing in the path. The soft green leaves would come home with us too, for throwing in a pot of water with chicken and spice. But my tongue was set on the flavor of sun-warmed plums. Candy and treats from packages could be had any old time at the store, but these plums only came around once a year, and once the trees were done, you'd have to wait. When the white bucket returned to the kitchen and boredom was forgotten, I sat on a kitchen chair, feet dangling below as I ate plum after plum after purple, sweet plum.

Years later, after I had finished high school and gone off to college, I nearly forgot about those plums. Time squeezed and compressed into the busyness of creating a life away from my family, away from leisurely drives to truck farms and backyard gardens. I forgot about how blue the world looked when I woke from a nap in the car. I forgot about the sunlight slanting through dusty windows to strike against the dark curved furniture carved in an older age. I forgot about those summer drives and the taste of sun-warmed sweetness on my tongue. I forgot, that is, until my dad called me one late summer afternoon and asked if we wanted some plums. He had a bumper crop and needed help to eat them all before they went to compost.

A few days later, my husband and I pulled up to my parents' house, and once again I was sitting on a barstool in the kitchen, feet dangling as I munched purple treasures, all sun-warmed and sweet. Rinsing another batch of plums in the sink, my mom told me that Uncle Sammy and Auntie Dora were the ones who introduced my parents to each other and later were sponsors at their wedding.

"When we built this house, Uncle Sammy and Uncle Fred planted the trees in the backyard," she said. "They brought us seedlings from their trees for good luck."

She went on to explain that neither of the men were actually uncles of either of my parents. Sammy was Mom's distant cousin and Fred was from her dad's hometown. They were both old timers, schoolboys who'd come to the States when the Philippines was still a protectorate of the

U.S. in the early 1920s. They'd made it good in America, first getting married and then buying their own homes where they could plant trees, a sure sign of permanence and prosperity.

Neither lived to see the crop Dad offered us that year, but as I sat listening to their stories, I realized that growing things was about hope for the future, of planting a small thing into good soil so the plant will grow up strong. Gardening was about continuity too, from seed to fruit to harvest and back to seed again, especially for a Filipino garden, because seeds and saplings were part of the community, a way to keep together. A way to stop the forgetting that comes of separation.

When my husband and I bought our own house a few years later, a low-slung Craftsman with enough bedrooms for our two children and us, Dad brought over baby trees from his orchard, the second generation of Uncle Sammy's trees. After the trees were planted, Dad explained how to cover the seedlings that first winter to help them survive.

"Take good care of them," he said. "And you'll have plums just like us."

As we stood near the seedlings, we watched the children chase each other up and down the lawn. I wondered how much of the day they would remember and if they would match their childhoods to the growth of our trees. Soon, we all hoped, they would pluck the warm fruit from the trees in their hands, pop them in their mouths to relish the sun and sweetness on their tongues.

Hot Oil, Monsoon Rains

It is customary for a typical Filipino housewife to cook good food. In fact, two of her utmost priorities in life are cooking for the family and caring for the children. – Elsa P. Olandres, *Philippine Cookbook*

Fall 2004

Sitting at the dining room table together, my husband Kel and I planned our weekly grocery list like two explorers planning a trip into unknown territory. We tried to guess at the terrain we'd find there, armed with new information about the pitfalls of certain foods we had once thought safe to eat.

Bread, rolls, crackers, pasta. These are the first things we knew Kel had to stop eating when he was diagnosed with a severe case of celiac disease, an intolerance to wheat gluten.

Soup, marinades, pasta sauces. These were things we would fix or use once without thinking, then halfway through a meal realize that we hadn't checked the packages ingredient lists. More times than not, he'd have to throw out his dinner and find something else to eat.

Frozen French fries, ice cream, granola bars. These were the things that seemed to be okay until we discovered that ingredients like "msg" and "modified food starch" could be code names for wheat-based additives. We learned the hard way that we couldn't trust manufacturers with listing exactly what they put into the foods we were buying. Even the smallest exposure to wheat would cause

Kel's stomach to cramp and his peripheral nerves to numb for days.

Alternatives to wheat-based foods were expensive and difficult to find in our small Northwest town. We scoured the grocery aisles for palatable substitutes for the simplest of foods. Breads made with brown rice flour or tapioca starch were novel at first, but lacked the texture of wheat breads. Some organic canned soups and bottled marinades lacked wheat gluten, while fresh unprepared foods were the safest to cook. We found that the best wheat-free pasta comes from Italy, Mexican corn tortillas were really corn-only, and that Thai food was our best bet for going out to eat. We discovered that, for the most part, Asian food was gluten-free if we substituted wheat-free tamari for soy sauce. Slowly but persistently we adjusted to Kel's new diet, exposing him fewer and fewer times to hidden traces of wheat. Over time, his gut stopped cramping and he suffered fewer weeks of paresthesia, a strange numbness that traveled like a ghost across his body.

Easter 2005

Explaining Kel's condition to my family during holiday meals required patience and repetition. No, he can't have the rolls. No, he can't have the pancit with the sautéed wheat noodles. The cheesecake has a graham cracker crust; he can't eat that either. My aunt offered saltine crackers as a substitute, but we explained that the steamed rice was just fine. My mother counted on the stir fried vegetables as safe to eat until we realized they've been cooked with regular wheat-laced soy sauce. My cousin looked lost because she didn't anticipate Kel not being able to eat her dessert and felt bad when he went without a treat to end his meal. We had to convince her not to quickly run out to the store for something else.

My husband hated the attention, having to explain over and over again, and I felt disloyal to him as I piled food after food on my plate that he couldn't eat. The first time I brought Kel to meet my family after we began dating, they were skeptical that he would eat Filipino food. My mother stockpiled baloney and white bread for him then watched in quiet amazement as he ate plate after plate of rice and adobo chicken. My grandmother watched him carefully and seeing his enthusiasm, guided him by the elbow to her favorite dishes. She beamed proudly as he dribbled soy sauce and vinegar on his lumpia rolls and munched them. She told my mother that he was a good eater and from then on, Kel was accepted as a member of our family. With his severe change in diet, though, he lost that simple, yet deep tie with my family. We had to pack foods for him on family vacations if we couldn't be sure that the local groceries carried things he could eat. We tried to be nonchalant about the changes while being vigilant about exposure. More than once our shyness to ask a relative how a food was prepared resulted in days of suffering at home.

Within a year of his diagnosis, we had our routine down pat. For every recipe, we would check the common ingredients first then look for easy substitutions. Slowly, we converted old family recipes from both his Euro-American roots and my Filipino roots to preparations he could eat.

Good old-fashioned Missouri BBQ chicken? Easy once we found the right kind of wheat-free barbecue sauce. Pancit noodles? Just substitute rice threads for wheat noodles and we were set. Fish sticks? Mochiko sweet rice flour and Pellegrino sparkling water made a crisp, yet tender tempura coating.

Gluten-free lumpia, though, the Filipino version of a Chinese egg roll, eluded us.

The filling wasn't troublesome; sautéed meat and vegetables seasoned with garlic and a little wheat-free tamari, but the wrappers were more difficult. Our local Asian food store had commercial lumpia wrappers available in their frozen case, but a quick flip of the box revealed the ingredients: flour and water. "Flour" meant "wheat" and when we asked the clerk about a wheat-free wrapper, she recommended Thai spring roll wrappers dipped in cola to give the right color. We brought a package home, but I was suspicious that their glossy sheerness wouldn't hold up in the hot oil. We made Thai spring rolls instead and missed the crunch of fried wrapper between our teeth.

Then I started to remember. The white edge of a wrapper curled away from the curve of a black-bottomed pan.

A child's memory: someone I knew made lumpia wrappers from scratch. I searched my cookbooks for recipes to make lumpia wrappers. I asked my mother and she was certain, as were the cookbooks, that the only viable wrappers were the frozen ones in the red-and-white box "available at most Asian groceries." I was certain, though, that manufactured wrappers were a new invention, that lumpia were made by hand from start to finish.

My memory enlarged. The pan was heavy and hot. The wrapper took only seconds to cook. Nearby on a piece of wax paper, a small stack of lacy-edged wrappers grew. Cloud-filtered sunlight filled the picture window above the table.

I remembered I was standing close enough to the pan to see the wrapper cooking, but not too close. The pan was hot, so I was told to keep away. Instead of leaving, though, I stayed. I watched.

The memory was old, I knew, because it came slowly and wasn't connected to anything but this need to find a solution. Every time I tried to linger in the memory, it slipped away as if it had never been there at all. I told my husband about the memory, and he asked me where the scene had taken place.

"Lola's house," I said without thinking. "My grandmother's house. She's the one who told me not to get too close to the pan."

For months I struggled with the memory, trying to recall the moments before the pan on the stove, to see how my grandmother made the wrappers, but the scene faded as quickly as it had emerged.

Spring 2006

At church, I discovered that one of the choir members took orders and delivered homemade lumpia to parishioners. My friends said her lumpia were perfect, tightly rolled and filled with deliciously spiced meats. When I found her before Mass one Sunday, I explained that I couldn't order her regular lumpia, but I wanted to know if she knew how to make lumpia with other wrappers like the ones for Thai spring rolls? No, she said, but was willing to try the spring roll wrappers. I could tell she was doubtful about the spring roll wrappers like me, so I asked if she'd ever made lumpia wrappers from scratch.

"My Lola made them. I remember," I said. She shrugged, saying she had always bought the wrappers, even when she lived in the Philippines.

A low table. A two-burner stove. A stool. A white smock. Brown hands wrinkled. A paintbrush and batter. The rise and fall of a dialect I never learned, was never taught.

Lola had the softest hands. I would sit in her lap and she would just hold me while my parents visited with them, the dialects flowing freely among them. My father spoke only Tagalog, the standard dialect of the Philippines. My grandfather spoke Pangasinan while my grandmother spoke Ilocano, the second-most-common dialect of the Philippines. When my parents talked with my grandparents, the dialects would fuse with English phrases that I'd catch, but adult talk is adult talk no matter the language. If I got impatient and squirmed on her lap, Lola would pat my hands gently and rock me back and forth like a baby. I'd trace my fingers along her knuckles and nails, feeling the difference between her hands and mine.

Lola emigrated from the Philippines in 1957 when my grandfather decided to move his family to the US after the Korean War. He was a Philippine Scout and fought in WWII, escaping the Bataan Death March in its early days.

My grandfather, who admired the American Dream, wanted his wife and six daughters to live that dream. Lola believed in the power of education, so she worked in a Seattle industrial laundromat for several years to supplement their income and send all their daughters to college.

Living in the Northwest was hard on their tropical bones, and, every Fall and Winter, they complained about the rain. They talked about how, in the Philippines, the monsoon rains were warm but relentless, causing flooding for miles around their farm 'back home.'

The brush loaded with batter moved swiftly across the black-bottomed pan and the wrapper sizzled. Hardly a breath passed and the brush was set aside. Soon the edges of the wrapper curled away from the pan and fingers delicately pinched the edge of the wrapper, lifting it away. The wrapper floated onto the stack, and she began again. Dip. Brush. Sizzle. Pinch. Lift. Stack. Again and again.

The windows of her kitchen sweated from the humidity.
Outside, it rained.
Inside, oil sizzled.

Summer 2006

My husband and I are decent cooks, but we rely on proportions and ingredient lists. Without Lola's recipe, we had to guess. She probably used flour, but did she use eggs? How much water was in her batter, or did she use milk, or leavening?

Closing my eyes, I brought up the memories I'd gathered and tried to remember her mixing the batter.

When nothing came, I realized I must have been in the other room while she prepared the batter and that I had walked in after she had started the task. My frustration hid the pain of missing her. Lola died in the mid-90s after suffering Alzheimer's Disease for ten years. I could have asked her to teach me when her memory was still clear, but what teenager thinks to do that? What grandmother thinks she won't pass on her recipes in time?

We scoured the Internet for clues. Every search for "lumpia" or "lumpia wrapper" or "lumpia recipe" suggested frozen commercial wrappers. I posted questions on comment boards and received replies that resembled the blank looks of my aunties and the Lumpia Lady – "I always buy the wrappers in the red-and-white box. Dunno how to make them. Sorry." I began to wonder if my memories were fantasies, that Lola never made her own wrappers, that somehow the knowledge of making wrappers from scratch had been lost.

Finally, on Google, a recipe for Lumpia Wrappers came up.

1 cup rice flour
1 cup water

Mix the flour and water together and blend well to form a smooth batter. Grease a clean griddle or frying pan very lightly. (The best way to do this is to use a piece of clean cloth or paper lightly moistened with oil and wipe the surface of the pan). Using a paint brush, paint batter thinly over the griddle or pan, working quickly. Remove the wrapper with a pancake turner as batter dries.

Rice flour and water. The perfect gluten-free recipe. Technology Lola would have never understood or dreamed of delivered her recipe. Two simple ingredients, cheap, perfect for the wife of a retired Sergeant living on pensions from the Army and the laundry where she worked. I saw her clearly bent over a stove worn and marred by brown oil spatters.

The stove rested on a foil-covered wood carving board that separated the stove from the low table. A cotton tablecloth decorated with bright images of fruits covered the table and dangled off the edge. Lola balanced a green plastic bowl with the lumpia batter in one hand, while her other hand deftly swept the batter over the surface of the crêpe pan.

I knew it was a crêpe pan because I heard her sparse English words as she spoke to my mother about it. It was an expensive purchase, the first Teflon pan offered at the PX, but the wrappers cooked without sticking. Swipe, sizzle, flick. Swipe, sizzle, flick. With efficiency borne of years providing food for her family, Lola made wrapper after wrapper, ready to be rolled and fried.

When I told my mother about the memory and the recipe, she said she didn't remember.

"Takes so long to make them," she said. "Then you've got to cook the meat and roll them up and fry them. All that oil! That's why I buy them frozen. All rolled and ready to go."

One moment my mother said my grandmother didn't make her own wrappers, and the next moment she said Lola did but then stopped.

Maybe Lola got tired of making the wrappers by hand. Her daughters, wishing to save their mother the work, brought her the boxed and frozen wrappers one day and she never went back to the hot pan on the two-burner stove. She would have been proud to buy the wrappers premade. She had made it in the US, and she could provide the food she loved to the people she loved, quicker, easier, the American way.

Now I, a US-born Filipina, tried to duplicate her native way. We looked at the simple recipe again, wondered if the wrappers were going to be sticky enough to stretch, yet not so sticky that the finished rolls wouldn't release from the frying pan later. We plotted out alternative batters just in case the first ones failed. We decided to buy a pan heavy enough to maintain the right temperature. We gathered and cooked ingredients for the filling, letting the batch cool in the fridge. It all came down to rice flour, water, and a hot pan. Lola would have been impatient with our doubts, would have taken things into her own hands and proven what we only guessed at. With her gone, though, I wondered if it was easier to just go without.

One Sunday Afternoon

The heavy pan is hot and ready. The batter in the bowl is thin like cream. I hold an empty measuring cup in one hand and a silicone brush in the other. Kel has already made two lumpia wrappers, and they sit on a white plate nearby. They look right, but he made them, not me, and I hesitate. What if I can't make the wrappers myself? What if

I can't follow in my Lola's footsteps and provide lumpia to my family like she did?

Nervously, I stir the batter and check the consistency again before I dip the measuring cup in and draw out a portion. With a tip of my wrist, the pale liquid pours onto the hot pan, and I brush it over the surface. The pan is too hot and the batter sizzles, clumping with each stroke. My stomach knots, feeling the failure. I dump the lumpy wrapper into the sink.

I stir the batter again as the pan cools, then hold my breath as I pour the batter and brush it into a flat circle. The batter stays thin and doesn't sizzle. The edges turn to lace. Micro-thermals form along the sides of the pan, and soon the wrapper edge floats away from the surface. Glancing at the center of the pan where the batter is thickest, I wait for the wrapper to turn transparent like the ones Lola made.

Feet planted as if in battle, I grasp two edges of my wrapper. Slowly, the wrapper peels free from the pan, no tears. I raise it high in the air to check it. Not a rip to be found. I gingerly set the wrapper aside in a cooling rack and stare at it like it was a long lost artifact. Past now present, I take a breath and begin again. Pour, brush, lift. Pour, brush, lift. My technique is different from Lola's but the result is the same. A small stack of wrappers ready for rolling.

Between Kel and me, we make six successful wrappers. Many wrappers failed because the pan was too hot or we lacked skill with brushing and plucking. We feel giddy as we roll ground pork, Napa cabbage, and garlic inside the wrappers. The lumpia crisps golden-brown in the hot oil. I arrange the rolls on a plate and place a sauce made of wheat-free tamari, vinegar, and garlic in a bowl nearby. We stand across the counter from each other, the lumpia between us.

"Ready?" Kel asks.

We bite off the tops of our lumpia just like Lola had taught us. The first bite burns my tongue in a familiar way, the flavors erupting new memories of Lola's kitchen.

Bright-yellow cabinets, speckled linoleum, the ironing board flopped open from its hiding place in a cabinet. Lola sits on a high stool, a steel bowl in her lap, beans snapping as she snips them with her fingers.

We pour spoonfuls of sauce into the hot lumpia and each take another bite. The sauce blends with the crisp wrapper and flavored meat, opening my senses. Memory layers onto the present moment again and I remember Lola's garden outside her kitchen, my grandfather bent over a shovel and the sound of my cousin's laughter.

I look at Kel, wondering what he was thinking, feeling. Half his lumpia is gone and his eyes are wide with wonder.

"Good?"

He smiles crookedly and wipes tears from his eyes, then nods.

I suddenly realize he's been missing Lola as much as I have, missing that little piece from her kitchen lost because of his condition. The crispness, the sizzling heat, the saltiness, and homey-ness. All those things, plus the filtered light through her kitchen window and her memory of monsoon rains, all wrapped tightly in a starchy embrace.

Chasing after Papang

My mother is two years younger than my eight-year-old daughter now is when the Japanese attack the Philippines. She is outside in the early December sunshine, playing with her five- and three-year-old sisters and my grandfather's sister. Somewhere inside a clapboard house nearby, my grandmother rubs her pregnant stomach, her mind on what time her husband will come home from his daily patrol. A common day for Wardville, the small neighborhood where dependents of the Philippine Scouts and US Army live and sleep.

My mother hears the planes before she sees them, their sharp roar coming from the north. Was she playing hopscotch on the dirt track in front of the house, or perhaps playing tag with her aunt? I imagine everyone stands stock-still at the sound, unsure. Fort Stotsenberg had an airfield, and the rumble of planes wasn't uncommon, but the noise of Japanese bombers would have sounded different, I imagine, more urgent, more strident as they flew in groups of twenty-seven planes, nine clusters in trios, like black birds in stiff formation, high in the sky. The bombs fall on the airfield first, blowing up grounded planes and pitting the runways. People scatter, screaming in terror while my mother points skyward, her sister Elsa jumping up and down beside her in agitation.

"So much smoke," my mother tells me later. We sit in her kitchen late one night. My children are in bed dreaming dreams while my mother tries to remember a nightmarish time, to wrap her adult mind around her child-self's experience. "So much smoke. Black. There were bamboo planes along the runway. Decoys or something. Covered in…what's that called? You can't see past it?"

"Camouflage?" I offer. She nods and points to me, a satisfied press to her lips.

"Yes. Camouflage. They were camouflaged, but it all burned."

Accounts of the day note that many of the pilots were in the mess hall when the bombing began and that only a few survived, the ones nearest the door who heard the shouting and ran out of the building.

"My mother came out and got us. She told us to put a wet handkerchief over our faces. They were afraid of gas bombs. My grandma was there too. She had a woven basket, her suitcase —" She traces the air with her fingers in the shape of a rectangle. "There was food inside."

My mother and her family ran to Jack and Jill Hill behind Wardville and spend the night under the branches of a tree. I ask her what kind of tree it was. She shrugs.

"A tree," she says. "A big tree with lots of branches. We didn't know if we could go home."

Could have been a Nipa tree, common in the Philippines and often used for building homes in a short period of time. Could have been a Banyan tree, but I dismiss this almost immediately. Spirits were known to live in gnarled roots and shoots of Banyan trees. My grandmother would have avoided it. My mother wrings her hands, trying to remember, and I realize that as a six-year-old, she might not have known what the tree was called and so never had a chance to remember its name.

"There were stars that night," she says. "So many stars. We didn't know where Papang was. He was on duty somewhere."

They return home after dawn the next day, and the adults hurriedly pack. The fort, their home since my grandparents married, is no longer safe, and they have no way of knowing when the Japanese will attack again.

"Did you see your father before you left for the province?" I ask.

She nods, her eyes looking past me as if she can see the small kitchen of her old home, the weak December light through the windows, the cans of food still neatly in the cupboards.

"Everyone was crying," she says. "So I was crying too. Papang says to me 'We might never see each other again.' And I wouldn't let him go. I was so scared."

Her sentences are short, the emotion of the moment still weighted even sixty years after the event, a young girl in a grown-up's body.

They leave with all they can carry and walk to town, where the train station is located. My grandfather does not go with them. Instead, he heads north with the rest of Troop A, 26th Cavalry. Their orders are to set up lines of defense from the Lingayen Gulf where the Japanese have landed foot soldiers and prevent them from reaching the Bataan Peninsula, where most of the US and Philippine Army are stationed. He will fight for almost five months until the order to surrender is given and the Bataan Death March begins.

But my mother doesn't know this as the train fills with passengers. Were they pale despite their dark tropical skin?

Did they tremble as they settled into their seats, regret a forgotten handkerchief or framed photograph left behind? Did they yell and shout or just cry into their sleeves, prayers on their lips? My mother doesn't remember but tells me she imagines everyone was very scared.

"Then we heard the planes again," she tells me. "And someone shouts that we should all get off the train, hide under the train cars." She snorts softly and rubs her nose. "They were afraid we would get bombed in the train, but there we were underneath. What if the train decided to take off without us? We would have been crushed."

The squadron of planes in their strange three-by-nine formation passes overhead toward the fort. The passengers are spared, but what about the soldiers still at the fort? Would they survive another attack? Bombs and strafing gunfire would become the stuff of their dreams, the music to their meals for many months to come.

It takes the better part of a day for the train to reach Tulin, where my grandmother's family lives. My mother doesn't remember much about those first few months away from the fort, so I must imagine what my grandmother was thinking and feeling. At age thirty-two she has a small brood of children, a husband fighting in a distant jungle and no way of knowing if her move back home is permanent. Her family makes them as comfortable as possible, my grandmother's sister letting them sleep on the floor of her house, then her brother moving them to his house a short distance away. When the fighting continues and the Japanese continue to press southward, it becomes apparent that my mother's family will be staying in Tulin for the long term.

"My *lolo*," she says. "My grandfather, you see, was very well-respected, I guess. They built us a house, our own house. A little nipa hut with room underneath for chickens."

"Who built it, Mom?"

"Everyone! The whole village came and in one day built us a house. Big enough for all of us. Right on the edge of my lolo's plantation. There was a big guava tree and a mango tree. I remember. They fell down while they still had fruit. We didn't starve during the war, but we didn't have much either."

I imagine my mother turning seven a month after the Japanese first attack, look at my own eight-year-old and try to see our life now through my daughter's eyes. My mother remembers her mother crying every night. We adults often think that children don't hear us when we think they're asleep, that their world isn't shaped by our emotions. My mother doesn't remember much about those first few months in Tulin, other than the town being different from living at the fort. She remembers, though, the day my grandfather escaped from the Death March.

"I didn't see him come in," my mother says. "It was dark. Probably night time. When I saw him, he was holding my mom. 'We lost,' he said. Then he collapsed. Malaria."

She shakes her head again. We don't know exactly what day my grandfather made his escape, only that it was likely in the first few days of the march, when the Japanese were far outnumbered by their prisoners, sometime after they realized they didn't have enough food or water to keep their own troops alive, let alone prisoners. Those who could not walk were killed where they lay. Those who tried to escape were shot in the back. Those who tried to save their friends were bayoneted. My grandfather didn't talk much about the war when I was growing up, but sometime during my twenties he decided it was time to tell the tale.

"There was a well," he told us, "and everyone was so thirsty, even the Japanese soldiers. We all rushed for the well. They were shouting for us to stop and they were firing on us, but it didn't matter. We wanted the water." He waved his hand as if trying to push others aside. "My friends and I, two guys, got to the edge of the jungle near the well and we decided to run. We ran and ran and ran. We thought they would shoot us, but I guess they were too thirsty. We ran until we didn't think they were following us. We decided to go in different directions. Maybe then one of us would make it home. I don't know what happened with them."

My grandfather struggled through malaria, then struggled against becoming part of the resistance.

"They came in the middle of the night," my mother says. "They beat him up, but Papang kept telling them no. He had a wife and children, he said. MacArthur promised to come back and save them, he said. I thought they were going to kill him."

Once I told a veterans' advocate about my grandfather, how I wondered if people would think he was a coward because he escaped the Death March and didn't join the resistance.

"He saved your grandmother's village," the advocate replied. "If the Japanese had known he was there, a Philippine Scout and U.S. sympathizer, they wouldn't have just killed him. They would have killed them all."

"The villagers were clever," my mother tells me. "You've seen those big mortars where they pound rice? Every house had one and when the Japanese would come, the first one to see them would pound their rice. Boom! Boom! Boom! Then the next house would pound their rice. And the next and the next, until Papang heard the signal and he took his bolo knife and a bag of food with him. He would go up in the hills like he was a farmer, as far away as he could from the village. We would all hide under the house with the chickens until the Japanese left. Then Boom! Boom! Boom! The pounding would begin again. All clear. And Papang would come back."

I try to imagine what it was like living the next three years in the province for my grandfather, the soldier who became a farmer, who waited for his commander to recall him to the fort. I wonder what it was like for my mother, who was ten when the war ended. Four years is a long time for a child, and I imagine that for a time, day-to-day living with the war was just that, living.

My grandfather died when he was 83, and my mother slipped into a deep depression. When MacArthur returned as promised, my grandfather set out for the fort once more to report for duty. He would serve as an MP after the war, then join the US Army officially to enable their immigration to the US. My mother hardly saw him throughout her childhood, and by the time he retired, she had married and moved to a different town. Even though she was the one to leave home, she always referred to her father as the one who was gone.

"Always gone," she says to me. "I could never catch up with Papang. When he left to join MacArthur, I wasn't sure he'd come back, no matter how many times those rice pounders would sound, you know?"

There are tears in her eyes, and I wrap her in my arms, a five-foot-four six-year-old, wishing for a sky filled with stars and a tree to shelter us.

Falling from the Sky

In the Before Times, say the elders of Bohol, there was no land, only endless sea, and the People lived in a great kingdom in the clouds. They were ruled by a Datu who had a beautiful daughter. The Datu ruled wisely and carefully, and everyone loved the little girl who played in the great forests and fields held in the sky by clouds.

One day, though, the Datu's daughter became sick with a fever. Her skin burned hot as the sun while her body shook like thunder and perspired like a terrible rainstorm, soaking her bedclothes. She refused to eat, and every day she became thinner and thinner. No herb or chant could cure the girl and the Datu feared she would die.

"What should I do to save her?" the Datu asked the Babaylan, the kingdom healers. They looked at each other, their brows wrinkled with worry, for all their knowledge and prayers had failed. Finally, the eldest Babaylan stepped forward and bowed low to the Datu.

"There is only one more thing you should try," the Babaylan said. "She must touch the finest roots at the base of the sacred Balite tree. The power of the tree is strongest at the root. If the Balite cannot cure her, nothing will."

Waking and sleeping were the same thing in the maternity ward of Kapiolani Medical Center. It was hard to tell whether I had fallen asleep or just blinked my eyes. Beside me, my husband Kel dozed in the pink vinyl chair that he had unfolded into a recliner after our late dinner. Behind the curtain to my left, my roommate snored softly while outside our room I heard the shuffle of nurses doing their rounds. Time passed unevenly. The sweep of the minute hand on the wall clock jerked and paused. Ten minutes felt like twenty. An hour felt like two minutes. Somewhere around midnight, I began disbelieving the movement of the clock hands.

What does a mother do when the laboring is done but her child is nowhere to be seen or held? Less than 12 hours earlier, I had unexpectedly given birth to a little girl we named Ligaya. In the neonatal intensive care unit of the hospital, she lay in an incubator while nurses routinely checked her vitals. Born eight weeks too early, they would be vigilant for any sign of trouble. Maybe she slept. Maybe she opened her eyes to watch the strange round, glowing light above her as it shifted in and out of her focus. Maybe she felt her fingers against her chin as her limbs moved of their own accord. She had no sense of time either, I suspected, but lacking any experience at all, she likely took it all in as one single moment. I was the one struggling to make sense of time and space.

The yellow taxi. The scent of disinfectant. The clatter of metal instruments against metal trays. Bright examination lights. All those moments adding up to a night in a hospital room where time tightened around pain, then loosened again around worried thoughts. How long had we been in Honolulu now? How long had it been since we left the little town of Moscow on the western border of Idaho? If my mind had been clear, my body rested, I would have remembered, but there had been no time to rest. We had arrived in Hawaii only eight days before, after leaving the mainland so my husband could attend graduate school at the University of Hawaii. With more time, I would have remembered handing the keys to our house to renters, closing the doors of our storage unit, and saying good-bye to our friends and family who wished us well on our adventure.

But in the dimly lit hospital room, I could only ask myself why we had left home, if what waited for us in Hawaii was all going to be like the morning of terror like we had just experienced. Moscow was a comfortably confining small town surrounded by wheat and pea fields, where winters were frosted with ice and summers baked yellow-brown with dust. We had lived in a turn-of-the-century house with white siding and an ancient apple tree out back. Our friends joined us last summer beneath that apple tree to recite A Midsummer Night's Dream during a picnic lunch. Other friends sold used books and lived in a renovated schoolhouse. Family lived close enough to visit after a day's drive, but far enough away to fondly miss them between visits. I couldn't help but wonder if we had stayed in that small town, perhaps Ligaya would have been born closer to her due date.

If my heart had been calmer instead of tight with worry for our not-quite-four-pound daughter, I would have remembered why we left. Kel and I didn't leave because Moscow was a terrible place to live. We left because we wanted a different kind of life, and when Kel was accepted to the Chinese Studies graduate program at UH, we fell in love with the idea of living our dreams in paradise. Life in Moscow was steady and predictable, sturdy like the basalt that rimmed each hill surrounding the town. And I felt myself, like basalt, slowly but steadily crystallizing under the pressure of routine secretarial work punctuated by the occasional writing class. Like a boulder rolling down the steep Lewiston grade to the Snake River, once we had set our sights on Honolulu, nothing, not even pregnancy, could stop us from moving.

It seemed like such a good idea at the time – be audacious, live your dreams, and everything will turn out rosy. Wasn't that the story I'd heard before? When I was a child, my parents told me that I could be anything I wanted as long as I worked hard and was a good person. What does that story even mean after months of planning, yard sales, box packing, and a flight that took me away from nearly everyone I knew and every place I cared about? Giving birth early wasn't in the bargain. We wanted our child to be adventurous like us, willing to take her dreams seriously and throw every bit of herself into making those dreams come true.

We should have seen it as a fever, a tropical fever that settled into our minds and made us blind to the comforts we had created for ourselves back in Idaho. Maybe then we would have seen the cautions in the old Filipino folktale about the girl who fell from the sky. It was a story I read the spring before we moved to Honolulu. The story was in a slim book of folktales I bought from a vendor at an Asian Studies conference we attended. At the time I thought it was just a story, a trace of a time long gone.

At the center of the kingdom, a great Balite tree reached toward the stars with great branches thick with green leaves. Its roots tightly held the dirt on top of the clouds so no wind would topple it. The Datu's daughter would play in and around the gnarled trunk in the days before her illness. It was fitting that the great tree would help the girl heal.

The Datu ordered that a hole be dug at the base of the Balite tree. Workers far and wide came with their shovels, digging the dirt away from the trunk of the tree, then deepening the hole so the roots were revealed.

The Datu ordered the workers to dig deeper so the fine roots of the Balite tree could be seen. When they were done, the Datu lifted his daughter from her bed and tied a rope around the girl's waist.

"I will lower you down," he said to his daughter. "When you see the Balite tree's finest roots, touch them, and you will be healed. Then, I will bring you back up again."

The Datu gently lowered the girl into the hole, but the workers had dug the hole too deeply and they pierced the clouds. The fingertips of the Datu's daughter brushed the deepest roots of the tree and she was instantly healed of her fever. She felt warm instead of cold. Her body no longer shook and sweated. Her muscles felt strong instead of weak. For the first time in months she smiled. But the girl was so thin from the fever she slipped out of the rope loop. She fell from the Sky Kingdom down toward the deep ocean far below.

"Father!" she called. "I'm cured!"

She looked up but instead of seeing her father's eyes welcoming her home, she saw the gaping hole in the sky and she realized she was falling.

Falling.

Falling toward the sea.

The Datu's daughter struggled to grab the rope that had slipped from her waist, but she was falling too fast. Her mouth opened and she screamed.

"Help me!"

My husband and I thought we had planned our move from Moscow to Honolulu so carefully. We sorted and packed, stored and sold all the things we didn't think we would need. We rented our house, left our jobs, and said goodbye to family and friends on the mainland. But like the workers who dug the hole too deep near the roots of the Balite tree, we strayed too close to danger, careless in our excitement, believing that the rope we had fashioned would hold us fast.

What was that rope woven from? At the time I thought it was woven from carefully written lists, budgets I created and reviewed with Kel, and calls to shirttail relations who lived on Oahu and who might help us settle into our new home. There were threads drawn from encouraging stories Kel's parents told us. They had lived the first part of their marriage in student housing at universities in the Midwest. They raised two children during that time, and Kel's mom held down a part-time job as a phone switchboard operator, typing up her husband's academic papers on an old Corona typewriter after work. Times were lean, they would tell us, but they found friendships that would last them a lifetime. Chili dinners together after football games. Young kids piled on coats in the bedroom, swapping comic books and taking naps. They were friendships that could be counted on, they'd told us, and thought that we'd find the same in Honolulu.

My parent's stories were similar, more strands drawn from their love of travel. As young immigrants, they pinned their hopes of future happiness on the Filipino community stateside. After a month-long voyage on the USS Barrett, my father met old-timers in Seattle who made sure he and his fellow Filipino Navy men would have a place to spend their Christmas, a place with foods from back home: pancit, adobo, and pan de sal. When my mother arrived in Seattle a couple of months later, it was those same old-timers who sent my father and his buddies over to the relatives with whom she was staying. It was her birthday and she was feeling homesick. She remembered my father because he was quiet and held the flowers they had all bought for her. They stayed connected to their community because their travels were supported by a series of connections where "Auntie" and "Uncle" were not about blood ties, but about being taken care of by the elders, the first ones who had made the journey to the new land.

My parents wanted to help us do the same in Honolulu. A lot of Filipinos lived in Hawaii, they told us, drawn to the opportunities of the military bases there and the sugar cane fields. They searched for and found friends of relatives that lived in Honolulu and told them we were coming. People we had not met yet were excited for us to arrive, excited at the prospect of Ligaya's arrival. But in the press of getting ourselves oriented to Honolulu we didn't call the Aunties and Uncles my parents had contacted, nor had we taken those phone numbers with us to the hospital. We didn't know how to tell them about Ligaya's premature birth.

Between dusk and dawn that first night after Ligaya's birth, I fell. Once I was like a child who trusted that everything that was happening would lead to a happy ending. I reached out, believing that I could be healed of the stagnation I had felt in Moscow. Then I would step into a new life in Honolulu, one I could make out of all those dreams and stories Kel and I had woven together. Instead, I found myself tethered to a hospital bed by an IV, falling and falling, wishing for wings to fly home.

I fell and there was no going back. No medication or prayer or fervent hope had kept Ligaya from being born. No way to recapture those two more months of growing for her or for me. After she was born, she looked so small as she peeked at me, all bundled and capped, her whole body fitting between the crook of the nurse's arm and wrist. How much bigger could she have been? How much more prepared could I have been to be a mother?

Cured of my tropical fever dreams of bliss in paradise, I fell, arms flailing in the wind. Uncertainty buffeted me like winds at high altitudes. The dreams I thought would come true receded into the sky like clouds. Downside up I fell, back flat, eyes wide, and no amount of scrambling to make sense of the days and weeks before the move would change the facts. I gave birth prematurely. I thought labor pains were just gas pains. I could not prevent what happened, no matter how much shock and denial registered in my heart.

Over and over my regrets tumbled, like the girl who fell from the sky, heels and hands flailing. The elders of Bohol said that there was no land beneath the Sky Kingdom, only endless sea. The girl fell and would hit the water, likely to drown for the lack of a mountain, an island, or even a rock – nothing she might cling to as she looked to the sky and the only life she had ever known. Thoughts of what could have been led me nowhere, just repeated themselves over and over, never landing me anywhere except where I was in the small hours of the night – a hospital bed, no longer pregnant, no longer fevered for adventure.

Perhaps the clock lurched again, or the nurse woke me when she checked my vitals, but I realized I was awake and thinking about the Datu, the father who thought he had done everything right to heal his daughter. Punishing the diggers would not bring her back. He had no wings to soar and save her. He had tried to heal her, to do the right thing, but like me, everything he did was not enough. All he could do was watch as his beloved daughter fell further and further away from him.

In that moment, I realized I wasn't the one falling. My daughter Ligaya was the girl who fell from my sky. The rope that tethered her to me was cut and she had slipped beyond my grasp. Separated by floors and walls and ceilings in a hospital, we were each alone, with no way to touch or hear each other breathe.

But the story does not end with the Datu's daughter falling into the sea.

"Help me!" she screamed, her hand outstretched toward the sky.

A small flock of ducks saw her first, surprised to see such a strange bird flying down toward them. Then they realized the strange bird was not flying but falling. Together they dove beneath the Datu's daughter, catching her on their backs. They were not strong enough to fly her home, so they landed on the sea. There, Turtle saw the girl's tears and called all the creatures to help. Rat and Frog. Toad and Lizard. Water Snake and Crocodile. They all gathered around Turtle and looked at the girl curiously.

"A daughter of the sky has fallen," said Turtle. "And now we must make her a place to live, for the ducks cannot carry her much longer."

The creatures all looked at each other and shrugged.

"What shall we do?" they asked.

"Someone must dive deep and bring mud up from the bottom of the ocean," said Turtle. "Then we will spread the mud on my back and the girl can live on the island we make."

Rat offered to dive first, but he could not swim far enough.

Lizard dove too, but she could not reach the bottom of the ocean either.

The Toad flapped his flippers and dove deep, deep, deep into the ocean. He was gone a very long time. At first, the creatures were afraid that he had drowned, but then he popped to the surface.

"Meers mud," he mumbled, then he spat the mud from his mouth onto the back of the turtle. Again and again he dove, bringing mouthful after mouthful of mud to the surface. The other creatures spread the mud over Turtle's back until there was enough land for the girl live on. Toad also brought plants from the bottom of the sea that grew into trees and plants the girl could eat.

The girl who fell from the sky became the first woman on the earth. She lived on the first island of the world, an island called Bohol.

My daughter, too, had her own beings to help her, kind nurses and doctors who caught her and gave her oxygen to breathe. They wrapped her in blankets and put a cap on her head to keep her warm. She was small and thin, just like the girl who fell from the sky. She may have slipped from my body, but she did not die, because there were people there to catch her. Like the Datu, I may have failed to keep her safe, but others cared for her wellbeing in ways I could not. Ligaya stayed in the neonatal intensive care unit for ten days, and we three lived in Honolulu for the better part of a year while my husband Kel studied at UH. We found new friends who enjoyed long talks over good food. Our family from the mainland visited when they could, and we met all those Aunties and Uncles we had heard about. Between midnight feedings and colic-filled nights were days spent together watching the ocean lap at the white-sand beaches, sharing halo-halo-style shave-ice in a town called Haleiwa on the north shore of Oahu.

Moving to Hawaii may have not started as the adventure we hoped for, but we learned that the story didn't have to end when things were at their worst.

With more than a little help from friends and strangers both, we made a new life on an island in the middle of the ocean. A life where we could look at the vast blue sky and remember a white clapboard house in Moscow, Idaho, where our child was conceived, then tell her stories about coyotes and ravens. A life where we could learn the stories of Maui and Pele, then watch Ligaya reach toward a rainbow arching the sky.

Later, I read to her the story of the girl who fell from the sky, then held her close. Babies grow into little girls who later grow into young women who search for their own adventures. Letting go is never easy, even for all the right reasons, but I hope the stories we have shared weave themselves into a rope strong enough to keep us connected, no matter how far we wander.

Kapwa Tao

Growing up in all-white schools in a bedroom community beyond the suburbs of Seattle, I never thought much about being other than what I saw — creamy-skinned girls, some with blue eyes, some with brown. Some shorter and stouter than me, some taller and more athletic, but we were all girls who wore red, white, and blue plaid skirts, white sailor shirts, and red sweaters, the uniform of St. Vincent de Paul School. We were all terrified of Sister Patricia, the principal, and we all loved Aries, the golden retriever who sat at our feet when we read books in the library. Being an only child, I wanted to learn the games the others seemed to know much better than I did, the jump-rope songs and hand-clap rhythms.

One cold November morning, I sat with two of my friends on a concrete pipe as broad as a horse. The cold surface stung my thighs, and the wind lifted my hair into my eyes, but it didn't matter much to me. My friends were teaching me a complicated singsong chant complete with hand gestures. They moved their fingers up and down on their faces, then brought one arm out and formed the fingers of their other hand into an inverted V, wiggling them as if they were legs. They waved a single pointer finger in the air dismissively, looked very serious, and then clapped each other's hands, missing on the last beat. They laughed and I laughed with them.

"Teach me," I said. They looked at me then at each other, then shrugged. I followed their movements as they slanted their eyes up and bobbed their heads.

"Chi Chi Chinaman, sittin' on a fence," they chanted. "Tried to make a dollar out of ninety-nine cents. He missed! He missed! He missed like this!"

I missed their hands just as they had done before and laughed. But they didn't laugh with me. They just looked at me, and then whispered to each other.
"Don't tell your mother we did that," said the blond-haired girl. The brown eyes of the other girl looked serious. "She wouldn't like it."

I shrugged and wanted to know why, but they wouldn't tell me. I tried to imagine why I'd get in trouble for showing my mother this new chant. There weren't any swear words, and they didn't say anything bad about God or the Virgin Mother. To my thinking, it was just a story about a Chinese miner, like the ones we were reading about in history class, who had a hard time making ends meet. I wanted to laugh about how we missed each others' hands at the very end, but somehow I knew that they wouldn't like that, wouldn't like me doing the chant with them. What I didn't know then and wouldn't know for decades, was this chant would be the first time I felt suddenly visible.

One moment I was an invisible girl on a concrete pipe, playing with her friends at recess; the next I was that girl of color who didn't know her eyes were already foreign and didn't need the help of fingertips to change their shape. They saw me in ways I didn't see myself because I yearned to be one of them – young, Caucasian, and belonging.

During the summer, my parents would take me to Filipino Community events, where I felt a different kind of invisibility and isolation. In the big community halls of Catholic churches or the Center House in Seattle, everyone seemed to have something important to do. Girls floated by in their Mestiza dresses while boys struggled to keep their Barong Tagalog shirts straight over their black pants. Everyone seemed to know the songs that were sung and the dances performed, while to me they seemed strange and outside my own life. No one spoke to me, no child approached me, and I followed my parents around as they visited friends. They spoke in Tagalog instead of English, and I found myself often under the scrutiny of someone I didn't know. They would ask me about school and admonished me to work hard to get good grades.

"She's getting so tall," a family friend would say. "And her English is perfect!"

My mother would nod and respond in Tagalog. They would laugh and look at me again. I tried to guess what was said between them, then watched as disappointment changed their friendly faces.

"But you don't know how to speak, ah?" the family friend would say as she shook her head in pity. "American born."

My father would tug his ear nervously and my mother would chuckle, then explain something in Ilocano to her friend.

"She doesn't have an accent," my mother would say finally in English, her voice slow as she carefully pronounced each word. "Better for school. She doesn't need Tagalog for school."

The friend would nod in seeming agreement and continue their conversation in Tagalog. I would begin to fidget, and my parents would send me to play with the other children. At larger family events, we child-strangers eyed each other warily. Cousins and siblings clung to each other, sharing jokes only they understood. The rise and fall of Filipino dialects at the event overwhelmed me and made me sleepy. I longed to go home and watch Gilligan's Island and The Carol Burnett Show on TV in the quiet of our rambler. When the singing and dancing performances started, I hung back from the others, unsure what the songs meant or why they seemed so important to everyone. They had all immigrated to the United States for a better life, so why did they keep trying to go back to the Philippines during these events? Once I was back in my familiar, nearly all-white school and parish, it was easy to forget see myself as a US-born Filipina. Being just an American girl was all I wanted. At least, that's what I thought as a teen.

In college I studied physics and mathematics, but also began looking for something I couldn't describe to myself or to others. In the early and mid-'80s, many of my co-workers at WSU's Residence Life and Housing were searching too and exploring crystals, channeling, and anything written by Shirley MacLaine. Once again I wanted to know what my Caucasian peers knew, but instead found myself the center of attention. Apparently my ethnicity was a sign of great inherent wisdom, and my friends and I were often disappointed when I didn't seem to know anything about Feng Shui or Zen Buddhism right off the top of my black-haired head. I threw myself into studying Celtic, Native American, and "Eastern" philosophy just to keep up with their conversations. I scanned bookstore shelves looking for anything about Filipino spiritual practices but my searches usually led me either nowhere or to texts about lost tribes who had no word for war.

After a few years of searching, I gave up on finding anything spiritual and indigenous to my heritage and continued living the borrowed life of a person of color passing as white. At one point I went so far as to create a persona based on a woman living in 15th-century Scotland in order to participate in a pre-Renaissance re-enactor's group called the Society for Creative Anachronism. Even travelling to the Philippines in 1995 did little to ease the longing my search had become, a longing of something that seemed both outside myself and inside at the same time. To me it seemed that after almost 500 years of colonization, there was little information about pre-Spanish spiritual practices in the archipelago we know commonly as the Philippines, let alone any current practitioners of those systems.

About 5 years ago I came across the term "babaylan" and the work of Leny Strobel. I found both soon after making contact with FilAm prose and poetry artists online. One writer mentioned the babaylan as a mythic figure in their writing, and I wondered if there was a piece of my heritage that resonated with what I'd learned from studying the indigenous practices of Europe, the Americas, and Australia. Others defined the "babaylan" as religious leaders, often women, who were warriors, healers, or psychic visionaries who were killed during Spanish colonization and all record of their existence had been erased. During my childhood, my family and Filipino community never spoke of babaylans, perhaps because of their strong Catholic faith. Were babaylans myth or truth?

If babaylans existed before the Spanish erased their existence from the culture, then maybe I could at least find stories about babaylans and reconstruct their practices by comparing them to what I knew from other cultures. When I contacted Leny she referred me to several texts, each difficult to find and requiring patience as the inter-library loan system shuffled books from one location to another. When the books arrived, I was disappointed to find that they were not easy texts to read, focusing more on the role of the babaylan in his or her community and not on the practices themselves. I wanted to know the words to chants, the names of herbs and stones they used, and where they traveled in their dreams. I wanted to see images of them in paintings and statues, or perhaps the objects they used in ritual, to have something tangible to confirm a deeper connection to my heritage than I ever thought possible.

In 2009 I was excited to hear that Leny and a group of others were planning an event designed to gather everyone interested in babaylans and babaylan practices together. The First International Babaylan Conference was her brainchild, and it flourished under her leadership. Like the rest of her work, the conference came about because of the community she created, the core planning group of women with the vision, skills, and dedication to turn a small corner of the Sonoma State University into a sacred place where FilAms and Filipinos could blink away the grime of not quite fitting in anywhere, could shed the cloak of nearly passing-in-order-to-survive, and raise their open palms to the sky to say Tao Po! I am a human being, as I am now, as I was, as my ancestors were, as we all shall be. She created a space where the practice of kapwa – the self in other – could be lived.

Before the conference, the different parts of myself and my previous experiences were like the jumbled tumblers inside a combination lock. From the moment I stepped into my suite and joined a small group of women who I would live with the next few nights, it was as if a tumbler of a worn lock would turn and fall into place. Then another. Then another. A song would be sung. Thunk. A passing prayer whispered. Thunk. A term, a chant, and passing conversation. Thunk. Thunk. Thunk. Pieces fell into place that I thought were forever separated because of time and circumstance. Each moment opened the lock that had been set every time I experienced a moment of disconnection from myself and my heritage while I was growing up. At the conference I learned that I just needed a reflection in someone else's experience to affirm all that I'd known before. I stopped second-guessing myself. I stopped feeling outside my own culture. I stopped holding back "just in case" it wasn't safe to be myself. I stopped feeling isolated under the scrutiny of others and began to feel visible in a new community as I expressed an authenticity of self I felt emerging.

I could at any moment join a song or a chant and not be told that I shouldn't share it with anyone else because it was a secret that wasn't mine to share. I could hear the dialects around me but never feel left out or pitied because I could not respond in kind. I could offer my thoughts on dream interpretation, community building, and sexuality without wondering if I had overstepped my place in the conference. There was never a sense of shame or apology about the knowledge shared at the conference. We all shed tears of loss as well as tears of recognition throughout the two days. And most of all we danced and sang together, not in nostalgia for something left behind, but for something discovered as a community, something that had never been lost or taken away by colonization and oppression. By the end of the conference, I realized that what I was looking for was here inside myself and inside the hearts of others. We celebrated as kapwa-tao, like-hearted beings, with a mission to heal each other and to be healed.

Source Material for Redacted Poems

Babcock, Chester D. and Babock, Clare A. (1963) *Our Pacific Northwest: Yesterday and Today*, McGraw Hill Book Co.

Barrett, Gloria B., Bartkovich, Kevin G., Compton, Helen L., Davis, Steve, Doyle, Dorothy, Goebel, John A., and Gould, Lawrence (1991), *Contemporary Precalculus: Through Applications, Analysis, and Matrices*, Janson Publications.

Behrens, Laurence M. and Rosen, Leonard J. (2014) *A Sequence for Academic* (6th Ed.), Pearson.

Callicott, J. Baird (Ed.) and Frodeman, Robert (Ed.) (2008) *The Encyclopedia of Environmental Ethics and Philosophy, Vol. 1*, Macmillan Reference USA.

Crow, Edwin L., Davis, Frances A., and Maxfield, Margaret W. (2013) *Statistics Manual: With Examples Taken from Ordinance Development*, Literary Licensing.

Deans, Thomas, Roswell, Barbara, and Wurr, Adrian J. (2010) *Writing and Community Engagement: A Critical Sourcebook*, Bedford-St. Martins.

Fansler, Dean S. (1921) Filipino Popular Folktales, American Folk-Lore Society.

Fasenfast, Harriet (2010) *A Householder's Guide to the Universe: A Calendar of Basics for the Home and Beyond*, Tin House Books.

Fish, Stanley (2012) *How to Write a Sentence and How to Read One*, Harper Paperbacks.

Grigson, Jane (2008) *The Mushroom Feast: A Celebration of all Edible Fungi, Cultivated, Wild and Dried, with Recipes*, Grub Street Cookery.

Hammack, Judd (1974) *Waterfowl and Wetlands: Toward Bioeconomic Analysis*, RFF Press.

Hemenway, Toby and Brown, Gardner M. (2009) *Gaia's Garden*, Chelsea Green Publishing.

Hirsch, David (1992) *The Moosewood Restaurant Kitchen Garden*, Fireside.

Horner, Bruce, and Lu, Min-Zhan (1999) *Representing the "Other": Basic Writers and the Teaching of Basic Writing*, National Council of Teachers.

Johnson, Jean (1992) *The Bedford Guide to the Research Process*, 2nd Edition, St. Martin's Press.

Kennedy, Mary L. Kennedy, William J., and Smith, Hadley M. (2011) *Writing in the Disciplines*, 7th Ed., Pearson.

Luard, Elizabeth (2013) *The Old World Kitchen: The Rich Tradition of European Peasant Cooking*, Melville House.

Lutkwitte, Clair (2013) *Multimodal Composition: A Critical Sourcebook*, Bedford-St. Martin's.

Macchiarola, Frank, and Hauser, Thomas (1985) *For Our Children: A Different Approach to Public Education*, Contiuum International Publishing Group.

Michaels, Walter B. (2006) *The Trouble with Diversity: How We Learned to Love Identity and Ignore Inequality*, Metropolitan Books.

Native Critics Collective (2008) *Reasoning Together*, University of Oklahoma Press.

Nelson, Melissa (Ed.) (2008) *Original Instructions*, Bear and Company.

Paley, Vivian G. (2000) *The Kindness of Children*, Harvard University Press.

Pojar, Jim and MacKinnon, Andy (1994) *Plants of the Pacific Northwest Coast*, Lone Pine Publishing.

Rawlins, Jack, and Metzger, Stephen (2008) *The Writer's Way*, Wadsworth Publishing.

Resnick, Robert, Halliday, David, and Krane, Kenneth S. (2001) *Physics, 4th Ed., Vol. 1*, Wiley.

Reyhner, Jon (Ed.) and Lockard, Louise (Ed.) (2010) *Indigenous Language Revitalization: Encouragement, Guidance, and Lessons Learned*, Northern Arizona University Press.

Traunfeld, Jerry (2000) *The Herb Farm Cookbook*, Scribner.

Acknowledgements

"Becoming a Woman of Color" originally appeared in
Writing it Real, https://writingitreal.com, 2008.

"Hot Oil, Monsoon Rains" originally appeared in
Conversations Across Borders, 2013.

"Kapwa Tao" originally appeared in *Community: Maganda
Magazine*, iss. 27, 2014.

"Falling from the Sky" originally appeared in *Kuwento: Lost
Things, An Anthology of New Philippine Myths*, Rachelle Cruz
and Melissa Sipin, eds., 2014.

"Chasing After Papang" originally appeared in *Hawaii Pacific
Review*, Tyler McMahon, ed., 2014.

"Gift of Plums" originally appeared in *Beyond Lumpia, Pansit
and Seven Manangs Wild*, Evangeline Canonizado Buell et al.,
eds., 2014.

"muskeg" originally appeared in *Noisy Water: Poetry from
Whatcom County, Washington*, Luther Allen and J.I. Kleinberg,
eds., 2015.

"The Water Will Flow Clean" originally appeared in *Peace
Arts: Poems on Peace and Justice, Vol. 1*, Carla Shafer, ed., 2016.

"Trespassing" originally appeared in *Peace Poems, Vol. 2*,
Bethany Reid and Carla Shafer, eds., 2017.

The author also gratefully acknowledges the support
and encouragement of the many wonderful writing and
academic communities she has had the good fortune to be
a part of, especially the English Department of Western

Washington University, the Rainier Writing Workshop, Northwest Indian College, Red Wheelbarrow Writers, Chuckanut Sandstone Writers Theater, Peace Poets of Whatcom County, and The Center for Babaylan Studies. Without these vibrant communities, this book would have never come to fruition.

About the Author

Rebecca Mabanglo-Mayor is a Filipino American writer, storyteller, and creativity coach. She received her MFA in Creative Writing from Pacific Lutheran University in 2012. Her non-fiction, poetry, and short fiction have appeared in print and online in several journals and anthologies. Her poetry chapbook *Pause Mid-Flight* was released in 2010. She is also a performance storyteller specializing in stories based on Filipino folktales and Filipino-American history.

CPSIA information can be obtained
at www.ICGtesting.com
Printed in the USA
FFHW020702220519
52598912-58079FF

9 781732 863606